FOCUS on Literacy

Name ______________________

Homework Book 5

Barry and
Anita Scholes

Collins

Unit 1

Direct and reported speech

In **direct speech** we use the actual words of the speaker, putting them inside **speech marks**.

The boy said, "I'm going to the library."

In **reported speech** we say what someone said without using their actual words. We do not use **speech marks**.

The boy said that he was going to the library.

In **reported speech** the present tense changes to the **past tense**.
'I' changes to 'he' or 'she', and 'we' changes to 'they', unless you are writing about yourself.

Change these direct speech sentences to reported speech. The first one has been done for you.

1. "Supper is ready," she said. She said that supper was ready.
2. He said, "I'm playing football." ______
3. "The bus is late," said Nadia. ______
4. "Tea's ready," said Mum. ______
5. "We are going now," Jack told her. ______
6. "We went to the vets," said Gill. ______
7. "I spent all my money," said Harry. ______
8. She said, "I'm too busy to play." ______
9. "I'll cook dinner," said Dad. ______
10. "I enjoy swimming," said Sam. ______
11. "I've lost my pencil," she told him. ______
12. She said "I'll help Jim do the cleaning." ______

Unit 2

Plurals

Most words form their **plurals** by adding **s**.

*kitchen**s***   *table**s***   *dog**s***   *window**s***   *lamp**s***

Words ending in **s**, **sh**, **ch** or **x** form their plurals by adding **es**.

*cross**es***   *bush**es***   *sandwich**es***   *fox**es***

1. Change these words to plural.

a) fish ______________   **b)** box ______________

c) chair ______________   **d)** bench ______________

e) witness ______________   **f)** lunch ______________

g) stitch ______________   **h)** dish ______________

2. Choose five of the **plurals** you have made. Use each in a sentence of your own.

____

____

____

____

____

Some words ending in **o** add **es** to form their **plurals.**

*tomato — tomato**es***   *echo — echo**es***   *hero — hero**es***

But other words just add **s.**

radios   *pianos*   *solos*   *kilos*   *zeros*   *banjos*   *memos*   *dynamos*   *photos*

1. Change these words to plural.

a) potato ______________   **b)** piano ______________

c) mosquito ______________   **d)** solo ______________

e) banjo ______________   **f)** volcano ______________

g) photo ______________

2. Choose four of the **plurals** you have made. Use each in a sentence of your own.

____

____

____

____

Unit 3

More plurals

Most words that end in **f** change the **f** to **ve** and then add **s**.

1. Change these words to plural.

a) loaf ____________ **b)** scarf ____________

c) half ____________ **d)** wife ____________

e) life ____________ **f)** calf ____________

g) knife ____________ **h)** leaf ____________

2. Choose four of the **plurals** you have made and use them in sentences of your own.

____

____

____

____

For words that end in **y** there are two rules.

If the letter before the **y** is a vowel (a, e, i, o or u) then add **s**.

If the letter before the **y** is a consonant change the **y** to **ies**.

3. Change these words to **plural.**

a) day ____________ **b)** key ____________ **c)** chimney ____________

d) baby ____________ **e)** journey ____________ **f)** berry ____________

g) lady ____________ **h)** family ____________ **i)** valley ____________

j) pony ____________ **k)** fly ____________ **l)** story ____________

4. Choose five of the **plurals** you have made and use them in sentences of your own.

____

____

____

____

____

Unit 4

Synonyms

Synonyms are words with **similar meanings.**

1. Choose a suitable **synonym** for **"break"** from the wordbank to complete these sentences.

destroyed snapped burst cracked smashed splintered wrecked crumbled

a) The soap bubbles _____________.

b) He _____________ the window.

c) The soft rock _____________ in his hands.

d) The thin ice _____________ under his feet.

e) He _____________ the stick in two.

f) The ship was _____________ on the rocks.

g) The explosion completely _____________ the building.

h) The post _____________ when he struck it with the sledge hammer.

2. Use a better word for **"pile"** from the wordbank in these sentences.

collection heap stack load drift

a) After dinner there was a _____________ of dirty dishes to wash.

b) The _____________ of snow almost covered the back door.

c) Jack has a _____________ of stamps from all over the world.

d) Mum was angry when she saw the _____________ of clothes on the floor.

e) The truck was carrying a _____________ of sand.

3. Use a better word for **"cut"** from the wordbank in these sentences.

gashed sliced clipped chop sawed mowed

a) I _____________ the lawn while Dad _____________ the hedge.

b) He _____________ his hand when he _____________ the wood.

c) When you have _____________ the bread, _____________ some wood for the fire.

Unit 5

Statements, questions and orders

Statement:
I am tidying my room.

Question:
Are you tidying your room?

Order:
Tidy your room.

1. Change these statements into **questions**.

a) I am going to the shops.

____

b) This work is easy.

____

c) I like chocolate.

____

d) It will be fine tomorrow.

____

2. Change these questions to **orders**.

a) Are you taking your sister to the park? ______________________

b) Will you be going to your uncle's today? ______________________

c) Do you keep your room tidy? ______________________

d) Will you be home for tea? ______________________

3. Change these questions to **statements**.

a) Has Carl finished his dinner?

____

b) Does she think we will win the match?

____

c) Do you know what you have done?

____

d) Are we too late?

____

4. Change these orders to **polite requests**. The first one has been done for you.

a) Take these books back to the library. Please take these books back to the library.

b) Close the door. ______________________

c) Help me carry this box. ______________________

Unit 6

Joining sentences

Join these sentences in an interesting way using one of the **conjunctions** in the wordbank.
Try to use a different word for each sentence.
Sometimes it may be better to put the joining word at the beginning of your sentence.

if so while since when because although yet after before

1. It was raining. I went out for a walk.

2. I needed exercise. I went jogging in the park.

3. Jinny finished her work. She sat down and read a book.

4. Rangit finishes his homework. He can go out.

5. She did the washing up. Her brother was tidying his room.

6. Angus played football. He had a shower.

7. She could not get in. The door was stuck.

8. There was no one at home. The postman left the parcel next door.

9. He washed his hands. He sat down for dinner.

10. He tried his best. He still could not do it.

Unit 7

Writing a report

Rewrite, as a **report,** these instructions for growing seeds. The report has been started for you below.

1. Save seeds from fruits, and collect ripe seeds from under trees. Soak the seeds overnight.
2. Use a pencil to make a drainage hole in the bottom of each yogurt pot.
3. Fill each pot with compost and make a hole with the pencil for the seeds.
4. Not all the seeds will grow, so put several of the same kind into each pot.
5. Water the seeds and place the pots in a warm, dark place. Cover them with plastic bags to keep the compost damp.
6. When the seeds begin to grow, uncover the pots and bring them out into the light.
7. Water regularly while the plants continue to grow. This may take a few days or weeks. If more than one seed has started to grow in each pot, remove all but the strongest plant.
8. When the plants grow bigger, you can make them more bushy by pinching out the tops.
9. When the roots fill the pot, repot your plants in bigger pots or plant them out in the garden.

You may find some of these words useful.

first next then after that when

How we grew our seeds

First we saved fruit and tree seeds and soaked them overnight in water. Then . . .

Unit 8 Proofreading

Proofreading means **checking** work carefully for mistakes.
Read through each passage carefully for mistakes. Then write a correct version.

1. Bill was catched running away from a broke window. "I didn't do nothing," he said. "It weren't me who break the window. Harry were kicking a ball about. He must of done it."

2. Jo and me went to the beach yesterday. I laid on the sand while Jo swimmed. When she comes out she said, "You should have came in with me. It were really warm." I tell her I can't swim. "Then come for a paddle with us," she reply.

3. When arrived to the picnic spot, we unpacked the food from the boot and got out of the car. Mum have made some sandwiches and cakes, which was delicious. When we have eaten we did a game of cricket, but we loosed the ball and that were the end of that.

Unit 9

Word order

Sometimes we can change the **word order** in a sentence **without changing** its **meaning.**

There was the smell of roses in the air. *In the air there was the smell of roses.*

1. Change the **word order** in these sentences, **keeping** the **same meaning**.

a) By the stream there was a grassy bank.

b) Leanne had pizza for her lunch.

c) A beautiful picture hung over the fireplace.

d) You'll play even better if you practise.

e) He sat down because he was tired.

f) Answer the phone if it rings.

a) ____________________

b) ____________________

c) ____________________

d) ____________________

e) ____________________

f) ____________________

Sometimes a change in the **word order changes** the **meaning**.

The lion chased the man.

The man chased the lion.

2. Change the **word order** in these sentences so that the **meaning** is **changed** too.

a) The girl watched the cat.

b) Jenny bought her mum a present.

c) Tara dusted while Jack washed up.

d) Gary borrowed Bill's bike.

e) Before he went to the shops he wrote a letter.

f) After he did his homework he played in the park.

a) ____________________

b) ____________________

c) ____________________

d) ____________________

e) ____________________

f) ____________________

Unit 10

Proofreading for spelling and punctuation

1. Read through this passage carefully. **Underline** each **spelling** mistake, and then write a corrected version.

A line of ants hurryed accross the grass, eech won carefuly folowing the other. They went betwene the flour beds, allong the path, and threw a whole intoo the gardin shed.

2. Rewrite this passage putting in all the necessary **punctuation marks**.

nicky went to manchester to do some shopping she bought shoes a dress some books and a present for helen she arrived home at 16 acacia avenue at nine oclock

3. Rewrite this passage correcting all **spelling** mistakes and adding any necessary **punctuation**.

It was toms berthday on saterday. He had a radio-controled car new football kit and a two books we went to his party and had a wanderfull time.

"Thats the best birthday party Ive ever had said Tom Thanks evryone for coming and makeing it such a speshull day

Its my birthday next weak and Ive invited Tom to my party.

Unit 11

Words which sound like their meaning

Some words **sound like** their **meaning**.

1. Add words of your own to each list.

Water sounds

splash drip

gurgle babble

____

____

____

____

____

Sounds made by creatures

neigh hiss

chirp hoot

____

____

____

____

____

Sounds made by objects

ping jangle

clink clang

____

____

____

____

____

2. Choose three **water sounds**. Use each one in a sentence of your own.

____

____

____

3. Choose three **sounds made by creatures**. Use each one in a sentence of your own.

____

____

____

4. Choose three **sounds made by objects**. Use each one in a sentence of your own.

____

____

____

Unit 12

Homophones

Homophones are words with the **same sound**, but **different spellings**.

pane

pain

sail

sale

1. Complete each sentence with a suitable homophone.

weak	week	tail	tale	tide	tied	right	write	son	sun

a) We played on the sands when the __________ went out.

b) Read me a fairy __________.

c) The __________ is shining.

d) Last __________ I went to Peterborough.

e) Take the first turning on the __________.

f) His illness left him very __________.

g) She __________ the package with string.

h) I'll __________ you a letter.

i) He is my father, I am his __________.

j) The dog wagged its __________.

2. Use each **homophone** in a sentence of your own.

a) sea ____________________

b) see ____________________

c) to ____________________

d) two ____________________

e) too ____________________

f) through ____________________

g) threw ____________________

h) peace ____________________

i) piece ____________________

Unit 13 Nouns

Nouns are **naming words** for people, places or things.

Most nouns are **common nouns**:

table

chair

house

garden *tree*

Proper nouns are the special names of people, places or animals. Proper nouns always begin with a capital letter:

Belfast *Rahena* *Rover* *Newcastle* *Australia*

Collective nouns name a group of people or things:

herd *team* *bouquet* *flock*

1. Sort each noun into the correct list. The first three have been done for you.

stone	Henry	audience	Surrey	hammer	nail	Ravana		
building	France	Sam	shoal	bundle	window	crew	army	
Brendan	troop	shoe	Helen	leaf	Hull	gang	book	choir

Common	**Proper**	**Collective**
stone	Henry	audience

2. Choose three **common nouns**. Use each one in a sentence of your own.

3. Choose three **proper nouns**. Use each one in a sentence of your own.

4. Choose three **collective nouns**. Use each one in a sentence of your own.

Unit 14

Relative pronouns

Who and **which** are **relative pronouns**. They **link** people or things already mentioned.

Who and **whose** refer to **people**. **Which** refers to **things**.

*The children **who** practised hardest won the prize.*

*The boy **whose** book was stolen was very angry.*

*This is the painting **which** I like best.*

1. Complete these sentences with **who, whose** or **which**.

a) This is a very good book __________ you can borrow if you like.

b) Will the person __________ has taken my pen bring it back right away!

c) The girl __________ younger brother has hurt his leg is most upset.

d) The dog __________ barked at us is a terrier.

e) The cup __________ you sold me has a crack in it.

f) This is the lady __________ lives next door to us.

g) This is my friend __________ father is a policeman.

h) This is the house __________ was struck by lightning.

i) Mr Jones, __________ daughter is in my class, has just bought a new car.

2. Join these sentences using **who** or **which**.

a) Mrs Hornby lives over the road. She is a very friendly lady.

____

b) She found an unusual ring. It had a large blue stone.

____

c) This is the shop. I told you about it.

____

d) The gorgons had serpents instead of hair. They turned their victims to stone.

____

Unit 15

Possessive pronouns

Possessive pronouns show **who** or **what owns** the noun: **mine, ours, yours, his, hers, theirs**.

Ours, hers, yours and **theirs** never have apostrophes.

This is my bike. This bike is ***mine****.*

These are their coats. These coats are ***theirs****.*

1. Complete these sentences with suitable **possessive pronouns**.

a) This is my lunch. It is _________.

b) These books belong to them. They are _________.

c) I am riding my brother's bike. The bike is _________.

d) My room is smaller than my sister's. _________ is bigger.

e) Your car is faster than _________. Our car is slower than _________.

f) This book is not _________, it belongs to me. It is _________.

g) This pen does not belong to Jenny. It is Bill's. It is not _________, but _________.

h) My writing is neat, but Rohena's is neater. _________ is neater than _________.

i) My pen is red, Olivia's is yellow and Ravi's is blue. _________ is red, _________ is yellow and _________ is blue.

2. Use each **possessive pronoun** in a sentence of your own.

a) mine ______________________________

b) theirs ______________________________

c) hers ______________________________

d) ours ______________________________

e) yours ______________________________

Unit 16

Constructing sentences

1. Rewrite these sentences, changing the words underlined so that they have an **opposite meaning.**

a) The ring was old and dull.

____

b) Climbing the tree was difficult.

____

c) He whispered a few words.

____

2. Rewrite these sentences, changing the words underlined, but **keeping the meaning** the same.

a) The news made her unhappy.

____

b) She talked him into helping her.

____

c) The children were as good as gold.

____

d) He came up with the answer.

____

3. Make these sentences more **interesting** by adding words of your own.

a) The lady drew a picture.

____

b) The dog barked at a man.

____

c) A car stopped outside a house.

____

d) The frog jumped.

____

e) The spaceship landed.

____

Unit 17

Joining sentences

1. Join these sentences with **but** or **because.**

a) We could not go to London.
The car broke down.

____

b) He won the race. He was disqualified.

____

c) He fell asleep right away. He was exhausted.

____

d) I wanted to go the party. I was ill.

____

2. Join these sentences with **who**, **whose** or **which**.

a) Joanna is a librarian. She is my friend's sister.

____

b) Tim's finger was swollen. Tim went to the doctor.

____

c) This is the boy. He broke the window.

____

d) That is the dog. It bit me.

____

3. Join these sentences in any way suitable.

a) He opened the door.
There was no one there.

____

____

b) He played football. It went dark.

____

c) We went home. The match was over.

____

d) He went for a walk. He needed to think.

____

Unit 18

Investigating words

Complete this word chart.

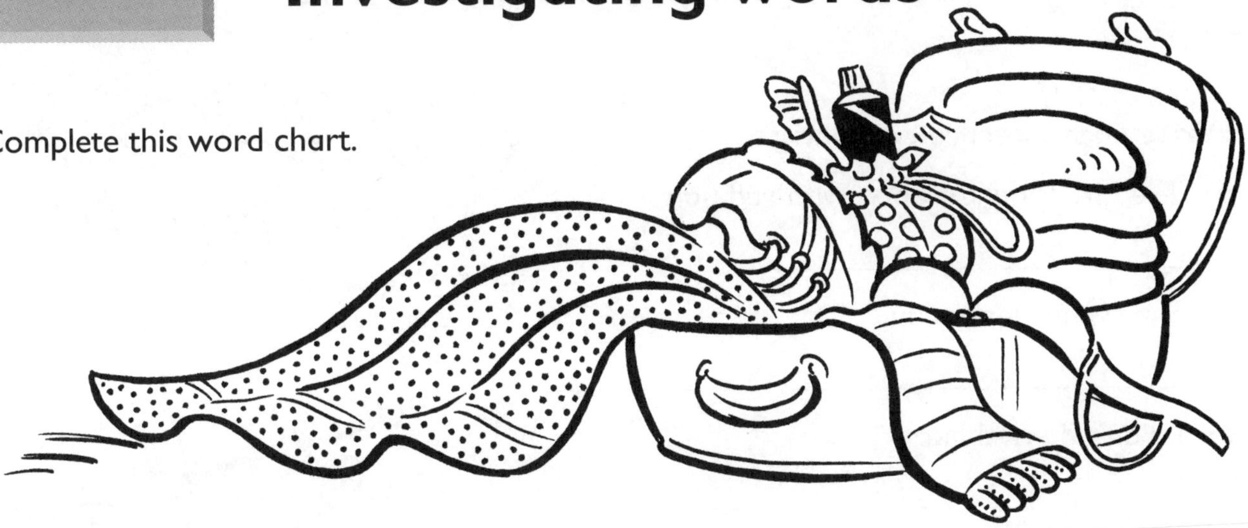

Word	Definition	Synonym	Antonym
full	no room for anything else	packed	empty
cold			
arrive			
thin			
clean			
true			
wrong			
start			
open			
rough			
pull			
early			
interesting			
hide			
rapid			
ending			
careful			
tough			
useful			
discover			

Unit 19

Correcting sentences

1. Write each sentence **correctly**.

a) The girl bought a book with red hair.

b) She swims yesterday.

c) I didn't do nothing.

d) We like cricket but preferred football.

e) Lee and Ben is going to Brighton.

f) I ain't coming with you.

g) He done it.

h) The boy owns the cat writing a letter.

2. Do the same with these sentences.
Write each one **correctly**.

a) He brung two apples and a orange.

b) It's time you go home.

c) He climb up and rescue her.

d) She had went for a walk.

e) This is the boy which helped me.

f) They sung a happy song.

g) There is six children in the group.

h) The sailor danced with a wooden leg.

i) I seen him broke the cup

Unit 20

Everyday expressions

These everyday **expressions** do not mean what they appear to mean.
They are **metaphors**, speaking about something as if it were something else.

have a feather in one's cap
(have done something to be proud of)

bury the hatchet
(make peace)

weigh anchor
(lift the anchor)

1. Match each **expression** to its meaning. The first one has been done for you.

let the cat out of the bag	act without delay
take forty winks	give up
strike while the iron is hot	stop suddenly
haul over the coals	tell what should be kept secret
throw in the cards	ignore
give the cold shoulder	sleep
pull up short	scold or punish

2. Explain in your own words what each **expression** means.

a) back chat ______________________

b) a dead cert ______________________

c) have one's heart in one's mouth ______________________

d) down on one's luck ______________________

e) lead a dog's life ______________________

f) sweep the board ______________________

3. Use each **expression** in a sentence of your own to show its meaning.

a) smell a rat ______________________

b) make one's mouth water ______________________

c) for a lark ______________________

d) pins and needles ______________________

e) playing with fire ______________________

Unit 21

Prepositions

A **preposition** is a word which **links two nouns or pronouns**.

The dog chased Tom around the tree.

She dived into the pool.

1. Complete each sentence with a **preposition** from the wordbank.

under through up over down next across beside

a) The girl climbed ____________ the tree and then jumped ____________ again.

b) She sat ____________ him and watched the birds ____________ binoculars.

c) He hid the money ____________ the rock ____________ to the oak tree.

d) The eagle flew ____________ the valley and ____________ the hill.

2. Complete the sentences about the picture, using **words and phrases** from the wordbank below.

outside under beside over in front of in on off behind inside

The fish is ____________ the tank. The tank is ____________ the table. The dog is ____________ the table. The TV is switched ____________. It is raining ____________. The light is on ____________. A picture is hanging ____________ the fireplace. A cat is asleep ____________ the fire. Another cat is sitting ____________ a chair. There is a bowl of fruit ____________ the fish tank.

Unit 22

Prefixes

possible → ***im**possible*

active → ***in**active*

1. Add **in-**, **im-**, **il-** or **ir-** to these words.

a) probable ____________ **b)** complete ____________

c) legal ____________ **d)** adequate ____________

e) replaceable ____________ **f)** mobile ____________

2. Find these words. Each word begins with one of these **prefixes**: **in-**, **im-**, **il-** or **ir-**

a) forbidden by law ____________

b) lacking in experience ____________

c) not logical ____________

d) writing that is difficult to read ____________

e) not costing much ____________

f) not pure ____________

g) easily annoyed or not wanting to wait for something ____________

h) doing things without considering the consequences ____________

3. Change these words to their **opposites** by adding a suitable **prefix**.
Write your own definition for the word you have made.

a) capable **b)** direct **c)** curable **d)** secure **e)** perfect **f)** edible **g)** frequent

a) ____

b) ____

c) ____

d) ____

e) ____

f) ____

g) ____

Unit 23 Clauses

In a sentence with more than one **clause**, one of them is usually the **main clause**. A main clause can stand on its own without another clause.

If it doesn't stop raining soon, ***the river will burst its banks.***

The **main clause** is ***the river will burst its banks***. This is because it makes sense on its own. The clause ***if it doesn't stop raining soon*** does not make sense on its own, and so cannot be the main clause.

1. Underline the **main clause** in each sentence.

a) When she found her lost bag she cheered up.

b) Even though she was tired she worked harder than he did.

c) I won't be able to see the stage if I sit behind Lofty.

d) Since she won the competition she has been a different person.

e) He climbed a tree when he saw the lion.

f) He washed up before he went out.

> Commas usually separate the main clause from other clauses.

2. Join these sentences. Choose a suitable **joining word**. Underline the **main clause**.

because although after unless when before if

a) He woke up. The telephone rang.

____

b) Call in. You are passing.

____

c) The river was shallow. It was still not safe to swim.

____

d) He went to bed. He put his pyjamas on.

____

e) They laughed at him. He was dressed as a clown.

____

f) She won't do any more work. She gets paid.

____

g) He washed the car. He went for a drive.

____

Unit 24 Using a dictionary

Dictionaries are useful for checking **spellings** and for finding the **meanings of words**.

1. Some of these words are spelt correctly, but others are not.
Use a dictionary to **check** each **spelling**.
Tick each word spelt correctly and write the correct spelling for the others.

a) heared __________

b) earth __________

c) freind __________

d) diffrent __________

e) follow __________

f) suddinly __________

g) baloon __________

h) through __________

i) stoped __________

j) somtimes __________

2. Learn the correct spelling of each word in question 1.
Use the **Look**, **Say**, **Cover**, **Write**, **Check** strategy.

3. **Write** your own **definition** for each of these words.
Check your answers with a dictionary.

a) important __________

b) garden __________

c) morning __________

d) clothes __________

e) hungry __________

f) stroll __________

g) joke __________

h) suitcase __________

i) shower __________

j) cottage __________

Unit 25 Abbreviations

Some words, phrases and names of companies, etc. are often written, or spoken of, in the **shortened form** known as **abbreviations**.

AAA → Amateur Athletic Association   *e.g. → example*   *CID → Criminal Investigation Department*

1. What do these abbreviations stand for?

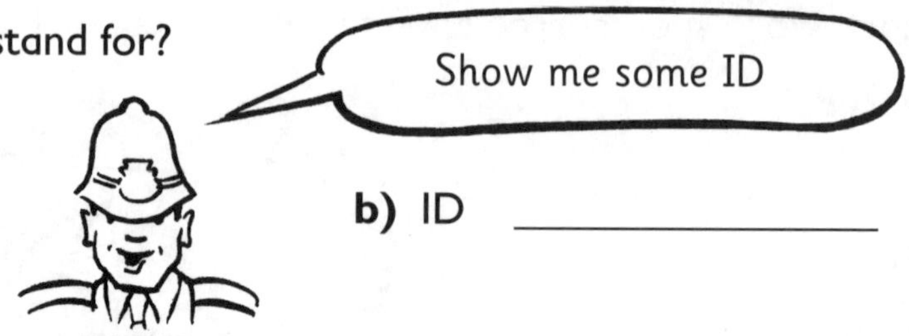

a) PC ____________________   **b)** ID ____________________

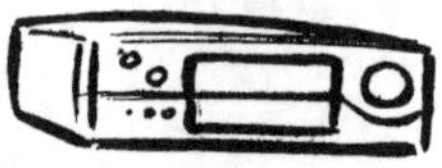

c) VCR ____________________   **d)** PO ____________________

e) RIP ____________________   **f)** DIY ____________________

g) BBC ____________________   **h)** ITV ____________________

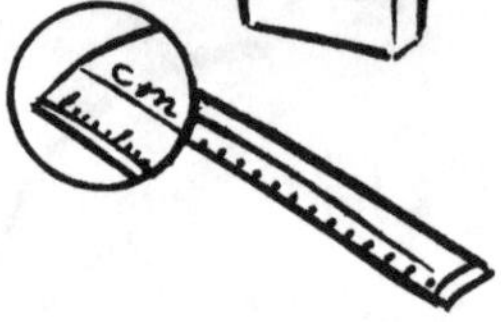

i) cm ____________________   **j)** kg ____________________

2. Write the **abbreviations** for these.

a) Football Association _______   **b)** read only memory _______   **c)** millimetre _______   **d)** millilitre _______

e) before noon _______   **f)** after noon _______   **g)** anonymous _______   **h)** His or Her Majesty _______   **i)** pence _______

j) His or Her Majesty's ship _______   **k)** parking _______

3. Use each **abbreviation** in a sentence of your own to show its meaning. Do it like this:

BBC   "EastEnders" is a programme on BBC television.

a) USA ____

b) WPC ____

c) UFO ____

d) CD ____

e) ITV ____

f) mph ____

Unit 26 Changing sentences

1. Rewrite these statements as **instructions**. The first one has been done for you.

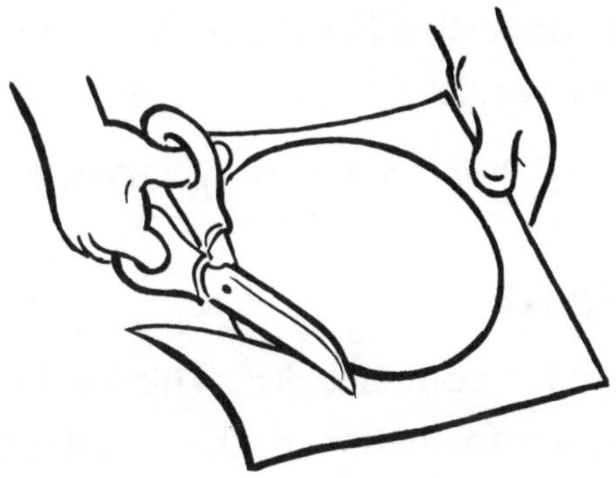

a) She closed the door quietly.

Close the door quietly.

b) He watered the plant every day.

____

c) Jake cut a circle from the paper.

____

d) He carefully unscrewed the lid. ______________________

e) She painted the room green. ______________________

2. Rewrite these questions as **instructions**.

a) Did you glue the picture on the paper? ______________________

b) Are you going to let me in? ______________________

c) Will you ring me when you get home? ______________________

d) Who put the box on the table? ______________________

e) Did you do your best work? ______________________

3. Change the **word order** in these sentences, **keeping the same meaning**.
You will have to change some of the words too.
The first one has been done for you.

a) He didn't like the book so he changed it.

He changed the book because he didn't like it.

b) It was a sunny day so he went for a walk.

____

c) He was so frightened that he ran home.

____

d) Riding a unicycle is not easy.

____

e) It is not a good idea to stay too long in the sun.

____

f) Eating too many sweets is bad for your teeth.

____

Unit 27

Words from longer words

Many everyday words are made from longer words. The words underlined in the sentence below are formed from longer words.

He bought a CD and caught the six o'clock bus home.

Acronyms

CD is short for compact disc. This kind of shortened word is called an acronym. An acronym is formed from the initial letters or syllables of other words.

1. What **acronyms** come from these words? The first one has been done for you.

a) radio detection and ranging radar ___________

b) North Atlantic Treaty Organisation ___________

c) binary digit ___________

d) random access memory ___________

2. Find out what these **acronyms** mean.

a) NASA ____

b) OXFAM ____

c) RADA ____

Missing letters

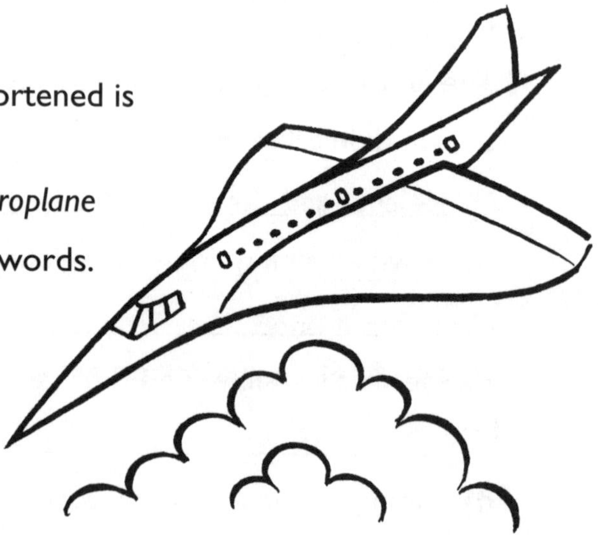

Another way some longer words and phrases are shortened is by missing out letters and prefixes.

Hallowe'en → *the eve of All Hallows* *plane* → *aeroplane*

3. Write the **short word** formed from these longer words.

a) of the clock ___________

b) telephone ___________

c) omnibus ___________

d) refrigerator ___________

4. Use each shortened word in question 3 above in a sentence of your own.

____

____

____

____

Unit 28 Slang

Slang consists of words and phrases used in **informal** writing or speech. Most slang words are short-lived. They soon fall out of fashion.

1. What do you think these slang expressions mean?

a) Spiffing!

____

b) Awesome!

____

c) Wicked!

____

2. A kind of slang still in use is **Cockney rhyming slang**. "Boots" are "daisies" or "daisy roots" ("roots" rhymes with "boots"). What do you think these Cockney rhyming slang expressions mean?

a) plates of meat ____________

b) whistle and flute ____________

c) Rosy Lee ____________

d) turtle doves ____________

e) titfer (tit for tat) ____________

f) Hampstead Heath ____________

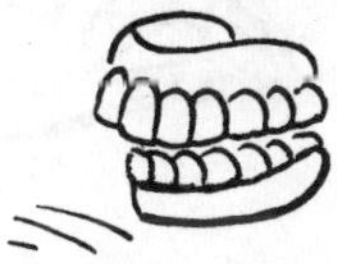

g) bees and honey ____________

3. These were once slang words. Slang words have now made their way into standard English. Write a **definition** for each one.

fun ______________________

flimsy ______________________

piano ______________________

4. What **slang expressions** do you use for these words?

a) very good ____________ **b)** very bad ____________

c) boring ____________ **d)** interesting ____________

e) money ____________ **f)** in fashion ____________

Unit 29

Proofreading: punctuation and spelling

1. Copy this passage putting in all the necessary **punctuation**. There are seven sentences.

it was a sunny saturday morning nina and i decided to cycle into the country we set off up sandy lane just past the village of downly we cycled along the canal tow path where there were fishermen
caught anything i asked
a few one of them replied
hope you catch more called nina

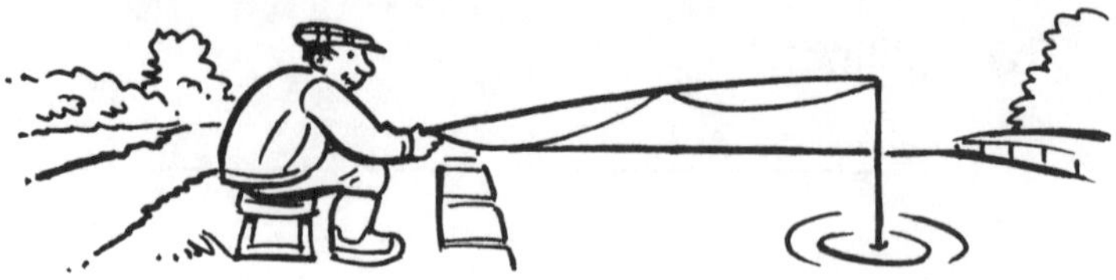

2. Copy this passage, correcting all the **spelling** mistakes.

Befour long we were hungry and thersty and stoped for snax. We fownd a plaice in the shade and openned our pact lunchs. It's funy how being outsied in the open hair maeks you want two ate and drink. Buy ten o'clok we had finnished all hour food!

Unit 30 Proofreading: standard English

1. Correct the mistakes in these sentences.

1. Many of the plates was broke.

2. Nobody are allowed in this room.

3. It isn't nothing to do with me.

4. The boys and Amanda was late.

5. One of the boys are telling lies.

6. Trisha could not do nothing right.

7. Has Deepak wrote this letter?

8. He has swam half a mile every morning this week.

9. Barney hided the watch where no one finds it.

10. Ben and Pete is going to Southend yesterday.

11. Everyone are going to the match who was on Saturday.

12. Nat and Nick is very proud to has been pick for the team.

Revision

Clauses

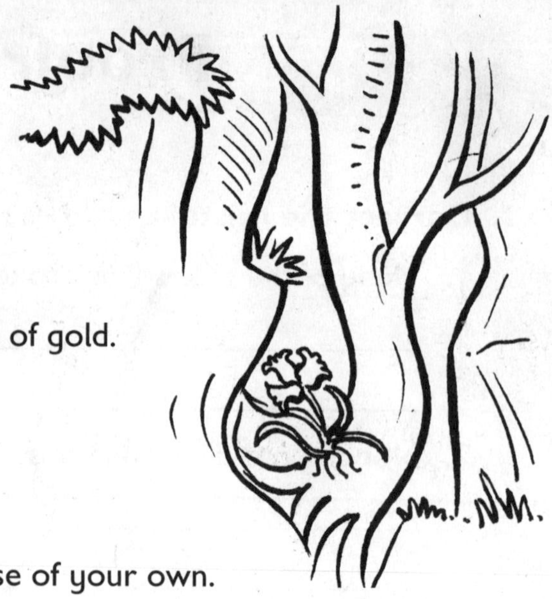

A clause is a part of a sentence. It contains a verb.

1. Underline the main clause in these sentences.

a) Arthur found a watch which seemed to be made of gold.

b) The rare flower grew where no one ever went.

c) We will go when our work is finished.

d) If I can save enough money, I will buy a bike.

2. Complete these sentences by adding a suitable clause of your own.

a) She was halfway to school ____________________

b) Ginny is a girl ____________________

c) He stared in disbelief at the dog ____________________

d) Without looking where she was going ____________________

e) After a hard day's work ____________________

3. Combine each set of three sentences into one sentence.

a) I have no money. I hope to save enough money. I will buy Mum a present.

Although ____________________

____

b) The game was over. I went home. Mum had my tea ready.

After ____________________

____

c) Summer comes. We will go on holiday. We will go to the Bahamas.

When ____________________

____

4. Write four sentences of your own, with at least two clauses. Underline the main clause.

____

____

____

____

Design: Grasshopper Design Company; Amanda Easter
Editor: Janet Swarbrick
Cover image: Dan Gair, Tony Stone Images
Illustrations: Pat Murray

Published by Collins Educational
An imprint of HarperCollins*Publishers* Ltd
77–85 Fulham Palace Road
Hammersmith
London W6 8JB

First published 1999

10

Browse the complete Collins catalogue at
www.collinseducational.com

ISBN 0 00 302515 2

British Library Cataloguing in Publication Data
A catalogue record for this book is available from the British Library.

Printed in Great Britain by Martins the Printers, Berwick-upon-Tweed

ISBN 0-00-302515-2

9 780003 025156